The Animal Heroes of the Forest

ISBN: 9798392837458

Sello: Independently published

Made by:Gian Poma

Contents

PART 1

"The Great Animal Race"

In a magical forest, many
different animals lived: rabbits,
squirrels, hedgehogs, deer,
bears, birds and many more.
One day, all the animals
gathered in a clearing to decide
who was the fastest in the
forest.

The woodpecker suggested a race to determine who was the fastest of all. All the animals were enthusiastic and accepted the challenge. But there was a problem: what would the race route be?

The smart fox suggested that they run around the forest, but the deer and the hare said that it would be too easy for them. The raccoon suggested that they run around the lake, but the frog said that he couldn't run that far. After much discussion, they finally agreed on a route that would be challenging for everyone.

The next day, all the animals met at the starting point. The hedgehog was in charge of giving the exit signal. The animals ran as fast as they could, each with their own technique and running style.

The rabbit started out strong but soon stopped to rest. The deer ran like the wind, but stopped to get a drink of water in a stream. The hare started slowly, but then sprang forward at great speed.

In the end, it was the little mouse who reached the finish line first. The other animals were surprised and wondered how such a small and agile mouse could have won the race. The mouse explained to them that it had not stopped to rest or drink water, but had run all the way without stopping.

All the animals congratulated
each other for having
participated in the race, and
they celebrated with a big party
in the magical forest. Since
then, all the animals learned
that it is not about being the
fastest, but about having
perseverance and resistance in
the race of life.

PART 2

"The Unlikely Winner "

After the first Great Race of the Animals, the animals of the forest realized that they had a lot more in common than they thought. They had all worked hard to compete in the race, but in the end, they had enjoyed each other's company just as much as the thrill of competition.

The animals realized that they didn't have to be competitive all the time. They could work together and enjoy each other's company in a spirit of friendship and cooperation.

One day, the animals noticed that a group of humans were cutting down trees in their forest. They knew that they had to do something to stop the destruction of their home, but they weren't sure what to do.

That's when the clever squirrel had an idea. He suggested that they band together and form a blockade around the trees that the humans wanted to cut down. If they all worked together, they could stop the humans from destroying their forest.

The other animals were hesitant at first, but the squirrel's plan made sense. So, they worked together to form a blockade around the trees. The birds flew above, keeping an eye out for the humans. The rabbits and squirrels dug holes to trip up the humans if they tried to cross the blockade. And the deer used their strength to push fallen trees into the path of the humans.

The blockade worked! The humans were unable to cut down the trees, and they eventually gave up and left the forest.

The animals cheered and
celebrated their victory. They
realized that they were stronger
together than they ever could be
alone. From that day on, they
worked together to protect their
home and the creatures who
lived there.

And so, the animals of the forest continued to enjoy their friendship and cooperation. They knew that they could face any challenge if they worked together, and they lived happily ever after in their beautiful forest home.

The animals huddled together in fear, not knowing what to do. They tried to take shelter, but the wind was too strong and the rain was too heavy.

As the storm raged on, the animals began to realize that they needed to work together to survive. The birds flew to the treetops and tried to shield the others from the wind. The rabbits dug burrows for the smaller animals to hide in. The deer used their antlers to break fallen branches and clear paths through the debris. And the squirrels used their nimble fingers to gather food and supplies for the others.

The animals knew that they had to work together once again to restore their home. They set to work clearing debris, repairing shelters, and planting new trees.

Days turned into weeks, and weeks turned into months. The animals worked tirelessly to rebuild their home, and their cooperation and teamwork never wavered.

And finally, after many long months, the forest was restored to its former beauty. The animals looked around at the lush greenery, the chirping birds, and the scampering squirrels, and they knew that they had accomplished something truly great.

The animals of the forest had faced many challenges, but they had always worked together to overcome them. They knew that they were stronger together than they ever could be alone. And they lived happily ever after in their beautiful forest home, enjoying the fruits of their cooperation and friendship.

One day, a group of humans came to the forest. But this time, they weren't there to destroy it. They were wildlife researchers, interested in studying the animals and their unique ability to work together.

The animals welcomed the humans with open arms, showing them around the forest and teaching them about their way of life. The researchers were amazed by what they saw. They had never seen animals work together in such a coordinated and efficient way.

The humans decided to stay for a while and observe the animals in action. They studied their communication, their problem-solving skills, and their cooperation. And in the end, they published a paper about the animals of the forest, describing their unique ability to work together and overcome challenges.

The animals of the forest were proud to have their story told, and they continued to inspire others with their example of cooperation and teamwork.

And so, the animals of the forest lived happily ever after, working together to protect their home and the creatures who lived there. They knew that they could face any challenge if they worked together, and they continued to enjoy their friendship and cooperation for many years to come.